Little Miss Dancey Pants

By: Kourtni Mason
Illustrated by: Sharad Kumar

For information regarding bulk purchases, please contact www.littlemissdanceypants.com.

Manufactured in the United States.

ISBN: 978-0-9971051-2-4 (Paperback)
        978-0-9971051-3-1 (Digital)

My name is Addison . . .
Madam Queen Busy Body!
From a very young age, dance has
been my favorite hobby.

I sing songs really loudly and bounce in my seat,
while snapping my fingers and tapping my feet.

Mama says, "Oh, Addie! Sit still.
You will wrinkle your dress."

But, I just can't seem to give it a rest.

I skip and move and bounce and shake.

The joy I feel I just can't fake.

I don't care who's watching. I prance and prance.
Boys tease, "Look, it's Little Miss Dancey Pants!"

But, I was born this way. I've known dance for so long because Mama's a ballerina – graceful and strong.

She sways across the floor, leaps to the sky
and turns on one leg in the blink of an eye.

I will follow in Mama's footsteps. This I know to be true, which means that one day, I'll surely be a beautiful dancer, too.

Saturday is my favorite day of the week because I get to travel to the studio and watch Mama on her feet.

One day, Mama saw me in the corner trying
to follow her moves. I did not have them
all, but I certainly had the groove.

She asked, "What are you doing Miss Dancey Pants?" I said, "I want to be just like you. I just want to dance."

So, Mama turned up the music and led me to the floor.
As soon as I started moving, she could say no more.

The next day Mama enrolled me in my very first class.
I was so nervous waiting for the time to pass.

My teacher, Ms. Dianne, greeted me with a great big hug. She introduced me to everyone, including Karrington, my best bud.

The dancers took ballet, tap, and jazz together.
Each day I was there I had the best time ever!

Before long, Ms. Dianne named Karrington and
me the "Dancers of the Week." I couldn't wait
to tell Mama. She'd be so proud of me.

When it was time for our recital, we wore
pretty pink tutus with gloves and a bow.
I was so excited. I even had a solo!

Mama and Daddy were smiling from
ear to ear when I took my place.

As I performed my solo, the light shined brightly on my face.

I knew it was meant to be. For I was
a beautiful dancer, you see.

When the recital was over, the dancers went
to greet our fans. I spotted Mama and Daddy
and ran to Daddy's outstretched hands.

Eagerly I asked, "Did you see?! Did you see?!" He beamed with pride and said, "You were as beautiful as can be."

And Mama replied, "You're a dancer now, Addie. Just like me!"

But, I knew it all along. I laughed and skipped while holding their hands. Of course I'm a dancer . . .

I'm Little Miss Dancey Pants!

www.ingramcontent.com/pod-product-compliance
Lightning Source LLC
Chambersburg PA
CBHW040023050426
42452CB00002B/112

9 780099 710512 4